MW00694908

Gustav Klimt (1862–1918) était un peintre symboliste autrichien fasciné par l'art japonais et les formes féminines. Son *Portrait d'Adèle Bloch-Bauer I* (1907) est un magnifique exemple du style viennois *Jugendstil*. Avec le visage du sujet émergeant de l'arrière-plan tel un rêve lucide, ce portrait est d'une beauté envoutante. En 2006, il fut acheté pour la Neue Galerie de New York et fait désormais partie de la plus grande collection Klimt.

Gustav Klimt (*1862, †1918) war ein österreichischer symbolistischer Maler, der von japanischer Kunst und weiblicher Form fasziniert war. Sein *Porträt von Adele Bloch-Bauer I* (1907) ist ein atemberaubendes Beispiel des Wiener Jugendstils. Das Gesicht der Porträtierten tritt aus dem Hintergrund hervor und macht das Porträt eindringlich schön. 2006 erwarb es die Neue Galerie von New York, wo es Teil einer großen Klimt-Sammlung ist.

Gustav Klimt (1862-1918) è stato un pittore simbolista austriaco affascinato dall'arte giapponese e dalle figure femminili. Il suo *Ritratto di Adele Bloch-Bauer I* (1907) è un magnifico esempio di stile *Jugendstil* viennese. Un ritratto di una bellezza intensa, dove il volto della protagonista emerge dallo sfondo come un sogno. Nel 2006 venne acquistato dalla Neue Galerie di New York dove attualmente è esposto.

Gustav Klimt (1862-1918) fue un pintor simbolista austriaco fascinado por el arte japonés y la belleza femenina. Su *Retrato de Adele Bloch-Bauer I* (1907) es un maravilloso ejemplo del *Jugendstil* vienés. En este retrato de belleza evocadora, el rostro de la protagonista emerge del fondo como de un sueño. En 2006 fue adquirido para la Neue Galerie de Nueva York, donde actualmente forma parte de su amplísima colección dedicada a Klimt.

グスタフ・クリムト(1862–1918年)はオーストリアを代表する画家であり、日本の美術と女性の姿に魅了され、作品を制作したとされています。『アデーレ・ブロッホ＝バウアーの肖像I』(1907年)は、ユーゲント・シュティール様式の最高傑作の1つに数えられます。ぼんやりとした背景から女性の顔が浮かび上がってくる様子が、夢と自覚しながら見ている夢のようであり、いつまでも心に残る美しい肖像画となっています。2006年、この絵はニューヨークのノイエ・ガレリエにより落札され、現在は同美術館のクリムト・コレクションのうちの1点として同美術館に収蔵されています。

paperblanks®
SPECIAL EDITION

Klimt's 100th Anniversary ~ Portrait of Adele

Gustav Klimt (1862–1918) was an Austrian symbolist painter fascinated
by Japanese art and the female form. He was a member of the Vienna
Secession, an art movement dedicated to introducing foreign influences
into their work.

Portrait of Adele Bloch-Bauer I (1907), which took Klimt three years to
create, is a stunning example of the Viennese *Jugendstil* style. With the
subject's face emerging from the background like a lucid dream, the
portrait is hauntingly beautiful. In 2006, it was purchased for New York's
Neue Galerie and is currently a part of the largest Klimt collection in the
United States.

ISBN: 978-1-4397-5290-6
MIDI FORMAT   240 PAGES   LINED
DESIGNED IN CANADA

© IMAGNO/Austrian Archives – ARTOTHEK
Printed on acid-free sustainable forest paper.